Hedgehogs

by Kris Bonnell

This is a hedgehog.
A hedgehog has small eyes and a long nose.

A hedgehog has spines on its back.
Spines help keep hedgehogs safe.

This is a hoglet.

A hoglet is a baby hedgehog.

7

Hedgehogs sleep in the day.
They are up at night.

Hedgehogs eat bugs.
They eat fruit, too.
Some hedgehogs eat worms and eggs.

Foxes like to eat hedgehogs.

Some owls eat hedgehogs, too.

A hedgehog can roll into a ball to be safe. Its spines help keep owls and foxes away.

5

Sometimes things get stuck in a hedgehog's spines.